OVERTURNING *the* TABLES

THIS DO IN REMEMBRANCE OF ME

TERESA BARNHARDT

OVERTURNING
the
TABLES

TERESA BARNHARDT

OVERTURNING
the
TABLES

TERESA BARNHARDT

Printed in the United States of America
Copyright @ 2023 Teresa Barnhardt
ISBN: 9798857504574

Library of Congress Cataloging-in-Publication Data

Editing: SynergyEd Consulting/ synergyedconsulting.com
Graphics & Marketing: Greenlight Creations Graphics Designs

www.glightcreations.com/ glightcreations@gmail.com

Cover Design: Greenlight Creations - glightcreations.com

Published by: SHERO Publishing
sheropublishing.com
getpublished@sheropublishing.com

OVERTURNING
the
TABLES

TABLE OF CONTENTS

OVERTURNING
the
TABLES

TERESA BARNHARDT

Dedication

**In Loving Memory,
Carol Joyner Hatchel**

To my precious Mama, you are loved beyond words and missed beyond measure. I have been blessed by your hidden talents and gifted abilities with your poetic writings. Your poetry echoed scripture and your messages were centered around love. I get to honor you and share my favorite poem. I hope this reaches to the Heavens, just to make you proud. You may be gone from us, but forever and always your legacy will live on for generations to come. I love you and I miss you!

**Borrowed Time
By Carol Joyner Hatchel**

I live each day
as it passes by
Making the most of it
I always try
Because… I live on Borrowed Time
When each day breaks
bringing a new sun
I will try not to
leave anything undone
Because… I live on Borrowed Time
When the day ends
And night is near
I hope for another tomorrow
And nothing will I fear
Because… I live on Borrowed Time

Dedication

Claire Flintom Barnhardt

My dearest Mama Claire, because of you, this is where it all began. You unknowingly sowed a spiritual seed in me that started a God-given journey. That small seed eventually led to a powerful divine revelation. Thank you for sharing your wisdom and knowledge with me. It was from the power of your words that this book developed. I dedicate this to you. I love you!

Acknowledgements

David

I am grateful for your unwavering love. Thank you for your constant encouragement throughout this journey. Thank you for loving me, like Christ loves the church. I love you!

Layton and Cayden

You are my gifts from the Lord! May you always walk in God's favor and grace! I declare that you both will walk in the identity and authority of Christ and you will love and serve Him only! I love you guys! Numbers 6:24

Leslie Mitchell Lunsford

To my maid of honor and our living angel, there will never be enough words to express our gratitude towards you. You are such a precious gift to us. You so selflessly and willingly gave your organ away. To you, it was just a small thing, but to us, it was everything.

We are forever grateful for you and the sacrifice you made to freely give life. You are a true example of John 15:13. We love you more than words can truly express. Thank you for donating life! We love you, YAYA.

To My Heroes of Faith

Debbie Mitchell

Thank you for all the love and support and for molding me into the woman I am today. I could not have made it through life without you by my side. I was blessed because I was loved by you.

Carol Scott

It is because of you that I have experienced the unfailing love of Christ. I now believe the power of the words from your favorite song, *"When He was on the cross, I was on His mind"* Thank you for leading me to JESUS!

Barbara Lynn

You were such a great mentor and a spiritual mother to me. Your prophecy, that was spoken over my life, is being fulfilled. I will always miss hearing you say, "I'm in love with a man I cannot see."

Janice Sumner

Thank you for enduring the last few years of this manuscript. Your constant help and endless encouragement have been instrumental in launching this book. Thank you for pushing me to the end.

Foreword

The author here is a friend, a beloved sister, and an insightful pursuer of truth. This is a fascinating picture of one of the many wiles of our enemy who seeks to steal, kill, and to destroy as we strive to serve the Father acceptably in this world. From her awakening to the Lord's powerful presence at a conference in Alabama, to the progressive revelation of the deceitfulness of demonic destruction, this is an enlightening read and is worthy of honest and sincere consideration as to its merits and validity.

I encourage you to read carefully and prayerfully the following discourse. What God created for our blessing and health has been altered by man to our great detriment. Satan is crafty, but his devices are easily exposed by the Spirit of God. Many hours of devotion have been poured into it. May God richly bless your reading and enrich your life through it.

Rev. Michael A. Clark, BA, BSN, M.Div., MBA, Ed.D, Th.D.
President, Nashville Bible College

Introduction

I invite you to join me in my passionate pursuit to the heart of God. It was in the secret place where I encountered the presence of God and experienced a real spiritual awakening. The eyes of my heart were opened to the deep things of God. It was, by the power of the Holy Spirit, that brought a transformation in my heart, mind, and my innermost being. I received a personal revelation that challenged me to fully yield and surrender to Him.

In the process of my pursuit, God began to overturn and flip the table of my views as I communed with Him. I found myself intrigued by the hidden mysteries of God and gluten, the intruder. By His grace, He has allowed me to share some insights and bring to light the things that were hidden in darkness. In doing so, it has exposed the plots and schemes of the enemy and his attempts to destroy us and make a mockery of God.

My desire, as you read my personal journey, is that you too will gain an understanding and importance of your own communion with God. I pray, as you read, *Overturning the Tables*, that the Lord will open your spiritual eyes and ears so that you may understand the difference between the traditions of man and the heart of God. As I reveal Communion: the element of surprise, your heart will be turned towards His truth. Once the table has been cleared, it will be time to reset it!

Matthew 13:11- *He answered, "Because the secrets of the kingdom of heaven have been given for you to know, but it has not been given to them.*

OVERTURNING *the* TABLES

TERESA BARNHARDT

CHAPTER 1:

When Kingdoms Collide

Chapter One:

When Kingdoms Collide

I came to an abrupt crossroad in my life. I had hit rock bottom and came to the end of myself. I was indeed lost, in a dry, weary, lukewarm spiritual state of mind. I was stuck somewhere in the valley of the wilderness and lost between the world and the church. I realized I was a carnal, captive, so-called Christian fighting her way out of bondage.

The outward facade left me so empty on the inside. I was tired of pretending and living a double life. I desperately needed something more, something real, something different, something I had never experienced before. I was in need of a breakthrough. I was praying, fasting, seeking, searching, and doing everything that I knew to do. But, yet there was something missing. There was an empty void and internal battle deep within me. I realized I was suffering in silence and was as sick as my secrets.

I was exhausted from running from God and tired of fighting the war within; living like the world, while claiming to be a Christian. I was double-minded and unstable in many ways. The more I surrendered and sought after God, the more challenging it became. That battle came to a head when the two kingdoms collided. There was spiritual warfare between the flesh and the Spirit. There was a war within my soul. I was reminded of Galatians 6:12, *that we wrestle not against flesh and blood, but against principalities, against powers, against the rulers of the darkness of this age, against spiritual hosts of wickedness in the heavenly places.*

I found myself in a crisis when I titled myself as a Christian but never had a real authentic and intimate relationship with Christ. I realized I had a cracked foundation and I had only *found* religion. I was professing to be a Christian, but denying His power. I had no real identity in Christ, no authority, no power, no peace, no hope, and no joy. I had a true lack of self; I didn't know who I was, nor did I really know who God was. So, consequently, I did not know who I was in Him. But I soon found out.

As an immature believer in Christ, I had to learn that when your true and real identity in Christ begins, your identity crisis will end. Then, you will become who God has called you to be. That abrupt crossroad and the point of desperation led me in a massive pursuit of Christ. I sought after God with my whole heart and all that I had within me. He led me to Jeremiah 29:13 (NIV)- *you will seek me and find me when you seek me with all your heart.*

I could feel a stirring and a shifting taking place within my spirit. I began to see my life change when I finally came to the end of myself. In a broken state of my life, I finally let go and fully surrendered myself to God. I grabbed my Bible and it opened before me to Ezekiel. That was the moment His word leaped off the page and it came alive in my heart. it spoke directly into the fibers of my heart. My eyes were fixed on the big bold letters flashing before me in. Ezekiel 36:26 (NKJV) reads: *I will give you a new heart and put a new spirit in you; I will remove from you your heart of stone and give you a heart of flesh.*

That was the day that His word came to life and so did I. I said, *"Here I am Lord; have Your way. I fully surrender to You; I give you all of me for all of You."* I felt an overwhelming sense of love that broke through the scattered fragments of my heart. I received a spiritual heart transformation. God was preparing me for what He was about to write upon my heart, mind, and spirit!

I often prayed the scripture in Psalms 51: 10-19 (KJV), *Create in me a clean heart, oh God, and renew the right spirit within me.* There was a renewing in the spirit that took place within me. In the midst of the seeking and searching, I was overtaken by His Holy Spirit. Revelation 3:20 (NKJV)- *Behold, I stand at your door and knock. If anyone hears My voice and opens the door, I will come into him and dine with him, and he with me.* And He did just that! It's not only our prayers that stand knocking at His door, but, yet He stands knocking on the door of our hearts waiting to be invited in. I opened the door of my heart and let Him in and He opened up the doors of heaven so I could dine with Him.

In September 2011, I attended the women's conference called, "The Ramp" in Hamilton, Alabama. It was there that I had a *love encounter* with Christ like I had never experienced before. There was an awakening that happened deep within my spirit. The Lord called me out of the darkness and into the marvelous light, saved my soul, and set me free from strongholds that kept me bound. I was washed by the blood of Jesus and baptized and filled with His Holy Spirit. I had an Acts 2 experience! I went from a carnal, captive, so-called Christian to a blood-bought, born-again believer, walking in authority and the victory in Jesus Christ!

CHAPTER 2:

The Big Interruption

Chapter Two:

The Big Interruption

August of 2012 marked the beginning of my God-given journey. But, let me warn you of what may happen when you surrender, seek the Lord with your whole heart, and pray for the heart of God. I began to pray for His perfect and pleasing will for your life. During the year gap between my encounter, with Christ, to the start of my journey, I was led in the wilderness to be pruned and refined by the fire.

After looking back over my journey, I felt this chapter title was very fitting in describing what was going on in my life. My spiritual journey was made known to me as I fully yielded and surrendered to Him. After my encounter with Christ, I came to a place of a true and real spiritual awakening in my life. I was finally ready to give God my best *YES*. I heard the Lord saying, "Who shall I send?" I responded, "Send me, Lord. I will go." I felt so strongly, in my spirit, that God was preparing me for something so big that it scared me. Now let me confess, I had no idea what that big thing looked like. I just felt such a stirring in my spirit and a spiritual shift taking place. It was then that my lifestyle was about to change within the blink of an eye!

Now, let me remind you that my husband David had lost his job, and was in desperate need of a kidney transplant. My immediate hopes and dreams were for him to get a donor for the transplant or to receive a miraculous healing. God, on the other hand, had something else planned at that moment. When that big thing finally came, it surely wasn't what I was hoping or looking for or even close to what I was expecting. I did not expect this kind of *big interruption* in my life. Now, there is more to this story, so you will have to stay with me until the end, to see what God had planned and His real purpose for all the changes that took place.

Now, brace yourself for this big thing that I was not anticipating. I thought this was gonna be completely different. Maybe this is a good place to insert the drum roll, please... So here it is: **Welcome to my interrupted and unexpected Gluten-Free life!**

Yes, this was it... I thought for a moment, "Really God, you gotta be kidding me?! Couldn't it at least have been a kidney on a silver platter?! Hello God!!! I am desperately praying for a kidney, and you want to shift my life to a gluten-free diet, during a major crisis in our family?" All that expectation and excitement just vanished. I felt so deflated.

I was beyond disappointed. I would describe the feeling as opening a Christmas gift that you were secretly wishing for... just to find out it's not even close to what you truly wanted. I thought, "How can I possibly be excited about changing my diet and eating habits? This is not funny, God! It was not what I asked or prayed for. This, God, I do not agree with and

I don't think I heard you clearly. Dear Lord, I don't know what you are talking about, and I think you've got the wrong person, with all due respect."

I began to ask the Lord what exactly is gluten and how and why did it even pertain to my life?! I thought for a moment that this had to be a joke! I'm sure I had a Sarah laugh of doubt moment. The kind where you laugh under your breath and say, "This will not happen unless YOU do it!" Oh, my goodness, the questions that began to consume my thoughts. Little did I know the importance of this horrible word- *gluten* and how it would impact me and my family.

"I mean really, come on God. I don't like it and I don't agree with it!" I began to whine and complain. I even doubted and questioned whether the messages were from God. We already had so much happening in our lives with David losing his job, his health crisis, and trying to maintain life as usual for our twin boys. This lifestyle change was the last thing I needed to deal with. I honestly thought God was going to use me in a mighty way and launch me out into ministry. Needless to say, I was shocked at this revealing of His big plans for me. "God, let me remind you that I am seeking after you, but not this. I need you to answer my prayers, **but** not change my diet."

As I began to settle my emotions, I took a deep breath and calmed myself down, I realized that I had been praying for answers to current health concerns. It took a little time to surrender, but I exhaled and said, "Okay God, if this is what you have for me, I will obey." I began my research on this gluten-free lifestyle. I truly didn't think this was even possible and certainly something I didn't really want to entertain or accept. I later learned my husband's family had a history of gluten intolerance and his parents had been recently diagnosed with Celiac disease. I didn't even know what that meant or even realize some of the medical issues that we all were experiencing, at that time, could be related to gluten intolerance.

After thinking back, I remembered having our son Cayden tested for food allergies as a toddler, but there was never a mention of gluten. We weren't too familiar with gluten at that time. It wasn't too long before Cayden's twin brother, Layton, started developing similar symptoms that worsened over time. That unknown monster, gluten, was raising its ugly head. As time went by, Layton continued to experience numerous attacks with abdominal pain that became more frequent. One night, Layton had such severe abdominal pain that we rushed him to the hospital, thinking it was his appendix. After having these repeated episodes with him, our frustration mounted. I was getting so desperate to find the answer to this nightmare, that I began to cry out to God for answers.

Well, at least I thought we were desperate. The truth is, God told me something I didn't want to hear, believe, accept, or receive. At this point, we surrendered and decided to have both my husband, David, and our son, Layton, tested for gluten sensitivity. The battle worsened after we found the solution. It was like God was ahead of us and was showing us the answer! We became desperate and willing to try anything to determine if gluten was the cause of our health concerns, but honestly, from fear of the results, there was some hesitation to having them both tested.

On the day of the testing, all four of us held hands and prayed for God's perfect will for our family. In the process of waiting for the results, we ate everything in sight, as if it was our last meal and we would never eat again. Waiting for the test results was an ordeal. Finally, the day arrived, and we received the results we had anxiously awaited. Both David and Layton tested positive for gluten sensitivity. We knew, at that point, that we needed to make some serious changes, even though none of us were ready for that! I wanted to get clarification and further my knowledge of the results. I called the lab nurse to get some additional information. Along the way, I continued to doubt the need for change. I began to challenge the results; asking many questions to avoid the necessary change. The response I received, from the medical experts, was like what a couple might hear about a pregnancy test. The nurse nicely stated, "Either you are, or you're not." Well, the test results were conclusive. Both my husband, David, and our son, Layton, were positive, regardless of the percentage of sensitivity.

Ultimately, I was convinced that something was going to have to change, and it wouldn't be in my own strength. Even through the devastating news, I did feel it was God's perfect plan for us. I did believe before this time that God had already prepared me for the journey, but I still fought the plan. After a night of praying, weeping, and negotiating, I surrendered. It was so exasperating and exhausting wrestling with the truth. There was no need to seek permission, approval, or opinions from others. I quickly learned that we don't need others to confirm what we already know to be true. I knew this was His will for us. So, it became real, and it all began the very next day.

I got a cooler and a storage bin and cleaned out the pantry, refrigerator, and freezer; we were starting over! My prayer was not my will, but His will be done. Eliminating gluten from our diets was a huge challenge. We would have to trust God because it wouldn't be done in our own strength. We all prayed together and agreed to look at this shift as a positive, rather than what it currently felt like, a punishment. I wanted us to look at everything we could have, rather than the things we couldn't have… which were numerous! Once reality set in, I was an emotional wreck. We all felt like crying, and we did at times. It felt like I was living in a dream, constantly under a heavy fog that I waited desperately to be lifted.

A few days into it, I was repeatedly asking, "Lord, is this really you? How long will this last? Lord, when will this be over?" I was like a kid on a long road trip asking, "Are we there yet?" I quickly began to understand what it meant to crucify your flesh. You talk about stripping everything away! When we started living gluten-free, I thought for sure it was going to be a short-lived, temporary inconvenience. I just knew for sure I would give up, quit and quickly throw the towel in. Little did I know that I would need to strap myself in with pen and paper to journal the journey. So, buckle up because we were in for a long ride!

The weekend following the test results, we went to Charlotte, North Carolina, to visit David's parents. It was a very different visit; it was an educational time with them. They began to talk us through the gluten-free lifestyle that we were embracing and embarking on.

Later that evening, when Mama Claire and I were talking about gluten, she began to tell me about the history of wheat. She made the comment, "This sure isn't the wheat that the Pilgrims brought over." At that time, she gave me a book called, **The Wheat Belly,** so I could learn more about the genetic modification of wheat. As we were discussing this new change, David's father, whom we all call *Pops*, also gave me an article about wheat and said, "This man won a Nobel Peace Prize for genetically modifying wheat." Their comments and shared resources really got my attention. I had always admired their wisdom and enjoyed their stories, but what they shared, that evening, was a little different from all the other conversations for the simple fact that it directly affected us as a family. I did not take any of their words lightly. I did my own research to learn more about it. I took all the information I was given and went straight to God. I prayed and simply asked God, "Has the wheat been altered? What do you say?" I knew there were some spiritual principles and implications from this. He spoke Revelation 6:6- *And I heard a voice in the midst of the four living creatures saying, "A quart of wheat for a denarius, and three quarts of barley for a denarius; and do not harm the oil and the wine."* This provoked a question, when I read the great demand, *"do not harm"*. I had to ask, *"Does that mean the wheat has been harmed?"*

On our way home from Charlotte and our weekend visit with my in-laws, I told my husband that I felt like I knew a secret, a mystery, but there was so much more to it yet to be discovered. I even told him I felt like I was learning about something that was hidden. I thought about the passage in Matthew 13:11 when He told the disciples about the secrets of the kingdom of heaven. I felt something, in my spirit, that I couldn't fully explain. I began to pray for truth, guidance, wisdom, knowledge, and understanding. Indeed, I began to seek Him with many questions about wheat, and if and how all this was even related to His word and purpose for my life. This was so much more than just a medical concern; it was something deep within my spirit that made me pursue Him for answers.

Continue with me as I share with you about wheat and gluten and what the Lord revealed to me, as I sought after Him for the truth. I promise it will bless you!

CHAPTER 3:

A Field of Wheat That We Can't Eat!

Chapter Three:

A Field of Wheat That We Can't Eat!

U nfortunately, we have a field of wheat we can't eat. In the beginning, I had learned about the person that won the Nobel peace prize and the genetically modified structure of the wheat that is typically used and marketed. The discovery of genetically modified wheat was made by Norman Borlaug, the humanitarian hero, who was known as the "Father of the Green Revolution" because of his major contributions to increasing wheat yields worldwide. Due to his major scientific discoveries, Borlaug was also referred to by some as "the greatest human being that ever walked the earth." In 1970, Borlaug was awarded the Nobel Peace Prize, becoming known as the *Giver of Bread and Peace. Now that quickly got my attention!* It was documented that he had spent over ten years cultivating wheat. Borlaug believed and voiced that genetically modifying organisms would be the *only way* to increase food production during his lifetime. Did they quickly forget what God did when He gave manna from above and He used a raven to feed Elijah?

When I first learned about this man and the title He was given, I was immediately filled with righteous anger. Even though He did a great thing, during that time, I wished we could all agree that Jesus Christ is the greatest human being that ever walked the earth. He is the only one with the titles, *The Prince of Peace* and *The Bread of Life*. Borlaug was given such titles that only belong to Christ. Now allow me to share with you what I learned through my research and seeking the Lord.

Later, I was awakened, one night from my sleep, by His sweet presence and the sound of the words, *"I am the bread of life."* The next morning, as I happened to be reading in John, the scriptures about bread began to leap off the page! I found it quite intriguing that He speaks to me as to who He is, during my journey, as I am desiring to eat some bread. His words, in the book of John, reminded me exactly what He spoke to me. **John 6:48 (NLT)** - *"I am the bread of life."* and *John 6:51 (NLT)- "I am the living bread that came down from heaven.* If the bread, wheat, and wafer were altered, could it be a reason Jesus said, *"I am the true bread."*

Interestingly, Jesus was born in Bethlehem, which means, *House of Bread*. The Ancient Grain and the genetically modified wheat strains are clearly not the same. Wheat was the basic grain of ancient times. During that time, the people called it the "staff of life." Einkorn wheat was one of the first cultivated wheats and became a major component of the diet, which reduced the need for hunting and gathering. Somehow, along the way, it went from cultivating and harvesting grain to recreating it. Hybridization methods transformed this grain using many human interventions. These new wheat strains have been made available without any testing with the FDA. Genetic modification is a direct manipulation of organisms, by human intervention. Synthesizing is creating something by artificial means, which changes it from God's original design. This should raise the question, "Is this what God sowed to the earth?" His Word said to cultivate, not recreate, and not to genetically modify, through manipulation in a lab made by human hands. Is it safe to say a good grain has gone bad?

"Wheat has undergone a drastic transformation of something entirely unique and unrecognizable when compared to its original and yet we call it the same name, *wheat.*" The Wheat Belly, Dr. William Davis, 2011.

The very creation of things cannot be retrofitted through artificial means without permanent damage to the original design! You can change the soil without changing the seed.

Psalm 104:14 (NLT)- *You cause the grass to grow for the livestock and plants for man to cultivate, that he may bring forth food from the earth.*

Cultivate, not by artificial means or redesign through genetic modifications, plant yielding, hybridization, breeding, or crossbreeding. Yield is productive to bear or bring forth as a natural product, especially as a result of cultivation. We have slowly strayed away from the hand and dependence on God but rather on man. Where did we go wrong from cultivating to recreating? We have gone from the ground of the earth to the hands of man in a laboratory. We now have new genetically modified strains of wheat. Have we gone away from God's original design? let's look at Genetic Modification.

Genetically Modified: A Genetically Modified Organism- (GMO) is one that is changed from the origin, which is the original. Some have said it stands for- *God move over; we will take it from here.*

Genetic: is determined by the origin

Modified: is to change

Genetically Modified Organisms (GMO) are organisms in which the genetic material (DNA) has been altered. DNA is the genetic blueprint

Norman Borlaug became a part of Monsanto, the world's largest agriculture company. It is proven when you genetically modify something, you own it and no one else has rights to it. Monsanto owns the seeds, and therefore secretly got around the FDA without any form of testing. Monsanto introduced glyphosate-resistant crops, enabling farmers to kill weeds without killing their crops. Some crops are transgenic and genetically engineered to be resistant to chemicals.

Glyphosate (n-phosphonomethyl) glycine is a systemic herbicide used to kill weeds; a class of pesticides, it is known under the trade name *Roundup.*

Now let's break down Monsanto.

Monsanto:

"MON": variant of man, and abbreviation for monetary, money

"SANTO" means "Holy or Saint" in Spanish - **painted or carved wooden image (idol)** of a saint. Common especially in Mexico and the southwestern United States.

Hosea 4:12 - *My people consult their <u>wooden idols</u> and are answered by a stick of wood....*

I find it very interesting that in English, we pronounce it gluten-free but in Spanish it *translates as sin gluten.*

I will circle back to Hosea in chapter six.

I began to ask God is this true, if so, tell me what you want me to know. I asked Him to "just show me, lead me, do something." It seemed like my whole world was being surrounded and consumed by bread, wheat, and gluten. The only thing that kept coming to my mind in the midst was, "Is this truly from you God?" and "How does this even relate to your Word?"

I continued to plead with God, asking Him, "If this is from you, then you have to show me in your Word what this all means." I spent time in prayer and in His word, and I was led to the Parable of the Wheat in the Book of Matthew.

Overturning The Tables   Teresa Barnhardt

Matthew 13: 24-26- Another parable, *He put forth to them, saying: "The kingdom of heaven is like a man who sowed good seed in his field; but while men slept, his enemy came and sowed tares among the wheat and went his way. But when the grain had sprouted and produced a crop, then the tares also appeared.*

Wow! We had to be sleeping and lulled to sleep not to see this coming! I have never had a Biblical story leap off the page like this particular parable.

It was one night, while sitting in my closet praying, asking Him to show me in His word if and how the wheat was genetically modified, that I began to get guidance. I glanced at my Bible, that was opened on my lap, and saw these flashing words. ***Ezekiel 17:10 (NLT)*** *"But when the vine is transplanted, will it thrive?"* The definition for transplanted means "to lift and reset a plant in another soil or situation." Needless to say, I had another "wow" moment! Now this may not be that kind of moment for you. This scripture passage may not validate my revelation enough to become your revelation and that is okay. However, for me, it was thought-provoking!

Now the wheat that we can't eat has gone from the field, to the lab, to our kitchen tables, and now to the communion table of the church. This was the enemy's plot!

I had no idea of the journey I was about to endure. As I began to learn more about wheat and gluten, the parables led me on a long spiritual expedition. Now journey along with me from where it all began and let's look at gluten; our enemy that has raised its ugly head!

CHAPTER 4:

Gluten,
The Intruder

Chapter Four:

Gluten, The Intruder

This gluten-free diet was far more than I could understand at the time. At this point in the journey, I knew, without a doubt, this was not just a temporary inconvenience, healthy diet change, a medical concern, or a typical fad. It was much more than I could even grasp, at the moment. I continued to seek the Lord in prayer. I still did not understand the significance of gluten as it related to God's Word and purpose for my life.

I discovered that wheat was genetically modified, but I had no idea what that entailed. Throughout my research, I learned that you do not have to be gluten-intolerant to be negatively affected by gluttonized wheat. Gluten is a harmful substance, like tobacco, alcohol, and drugs. It can and will eventually affect everyone, at some point, to some degree because of what it is. I only knew that I was doing something that was not in my plans, will, might, or power.

I was still in pursuit to find out why it was God's plan for our lives. I was on a mission to find out everything I possibly could about wheat, and gluten. I felt like there was something more that I needed to know, something yet to be revealed. As I said in the beginning, I felt like it was a secret of something hidden, a great mystery. The more I learned the more I desired to know. I knew that God, in His time, would reveal the truth and unveil what He wanted me to see. I guess you could say I was in hot pursuit of something. The unknown will certainly keep you searching. After learning all about the history of ancient wheat and genetic modifications, I still was unaware of the mystery of gluten. This horrible word *gluten* just began to sound like something I did not want to have any part of. I found myself truly surprised by what I began to learn about gluten. It is responsible for wreaking havoc in people's lives! It is an unnatural toxic substance.

Here are some important terms associated with gluten:

Gluten (Latin for "glue") is a protein found in wheat, barley, and rye. Gluten can create a super inflammatory response that can send off a body-wide infection. It has been documented to affect every organ in the human body. Gluten triggers inflammation and leads to numerous medical conditions and neurological issues. Gluten is absorbed in the bloodstream and makes it across the **blood-brain barrier**. Now, this made me think about the power of the blood of Jesus and how absolutely nothing can cross the bloodline.

Gluten *"glue"* is a tenacious elastic protein substance, found especially in wheat flour, to give cohesiveness to dough. Gluten is a sticky protein that holds bread together and allows it to rise. It gives elasticity to dough and acts like yeast.

Glutamine is also called *glutelin* or *glutenin*, a major protein in wheat that consists of two major sub-categories: gliadins and glutenins. These proteins also break down to glutamate.

Glutenin WGA (wheat germ agglutinin) is the highest concentration in whole wheat in the seed of the wheat plant.

Agglutinin is a substance (antibody) producing agglutination. Agglutinating is an adhesive, to adhere to, fasten, and glue.

Gliadin is a Prolamin derived from gluten. The glycoprotein" is a **Prolamin** derived from gluten. Prolamin is a protein in wheat that contains a toxic factor that is associated with celiac. Prolamin is a group of plant proteins found in the seeds of some grains.

Laminin the **"glycoprotein"** is a major constituent of a basement membrane that consists of three chains bound to each other into a **cross-shaped molecule**; laminins are major proteins.

They are two different kinds of proteins. One protein imposing like the other. But one is a toxic factor related to gluten and the other protein is the cross-shaped molecule and basement of our membrane. That is deep down to the very core of who we are. When I learned that gluten is the glue that holds the bread together, I immediately thought about Louie Giglio and his message about Laminin.

Laminins (glycoprotein) is the glue that holds our bodies together which is a glycoprotein that resembles the shape of a cross which only God could have designed in our human bodies. https://g.co/kgs/wE9NT1.

Prolamin (glycoprotein) is derived from gluten which is the glue that holds the bread together. I find it very interesting how these are the same, yet so different in so many ways. ***Both are glycoproteins and work as glue; one cross shape that holds the body together, and the other holds the bread together.*** One made by God and the other made by man. Remember there is always a counterfeit to the real thing. ***Colossians 1:17-*** *He is before all things, and in him all things hold together.*

I mentioned earlier that gluten can make it across the blood-brain barrier. Now, let's take a quick peep at the two different glutamates. **Glutamate** is derived from the proteins of glutenin.

Glutamate (Glu) is also a major excitatory neurotransmitter in our brain. Glutamate is also a salt of glutamic acid, known as MSG. Glutamate is an example of a neurotoxin.

Neurotoxin is a poisonous substance that damages tissues within the central nervous system. One example of a neurotoxin is the venom of some snakes.

After thinking and pondering on the negative effects of gluten I asked yet another big question, "What is strong enough to break the barrier of our intestines? And, what and how does it give food permission to roam about our bodies? I was eager to know what could possibly penetrate through the walls of our intestines to cause an autoimmune response in our bodies. I began to question God, asking Him, "If you perfectly designed our bodies from intake to output, what could break the barrier of our intestinal lining?"

I believe food was not meant to freely roam within our bodies. I thought, why not ask the One who created our bodies? I later learned that I asked the same question that doctors had just discovered after researching for many years. I was completely shocked and surprised when I stumbled across this information.

Modified wheat is a protein, and ancient wheat is a grain. There is a glycoprotein in modified wheat that activates **Zonulin,** leading to increased intestinal permeability. Gliadin derives from Gluten. Gliadin is resistant to human digestion. I began to ask God a lot of questions for answers I was not sure I wanted to hear. I continued searching for the truth and understanding.

<u>Zonulin</u> is known as our intestinal gatekeeper. It is a protein of tight junctions between the cells of the wall of the digestive tract.

The release of Zonulin will make the gut more permeable to molecules, allowing gluten access to the rest of the body. This triggers an autoimmune response and identifies **gluten as an intruder**. The gatekeeper has failed! The body responds with an attack targeting the intestines instead of targeting the intruder gluten. It also sets off an autoimmunity in your body against itself.

The elevated production of Zonulin affects the permeability of the blood-brain barrier and the lining of the gut. Zonulin is referred to as the **"adversary antagonist"** which I find very fitting from what I have learned. Who is our real adversary? Gluten is just like sin, with the negative effects that it can bring to our bodies.

Our intestines have tiny little hairs called villi. The villi are what absorb the nutrients from the digestion of the food. Gluten has been known to shave down the villi so it will no longer absorb the nutrients. It then breaks the tight junction (TJ) to allow passage through the walls of the intestines. TJ is the tight junction connectors between the intestines. Zonulin is a human protein that acts like a traffic conductor for the body's tissue by opening spaces between the cells, allowing certain proteins to pass through. When our conductor and gatekeeper fail, the protein gluten can pass through the cells in the intestines, triggering an autoimmune response. There again, food partials weren't meant to freely roam about our bodies. Many individuals, including myself, could never understand how gluten proteins could penetrate the human immune system. Gluten is known for infiltrating the lining of the walls of our intestines. Now let me show you what I discovered about Gluten, the big protein!

Shortly after learning about gluten, I still suspected there were some spiritual implications to this journey God was carrying me on. I often questioned why He brought this into my life, but I stayed the course. I wished I was able to fully express and put emphasis on the stirring that was taking place in my spirit. Before this journey began, I was really seeking after God with my whole heart and desired His will for my life. I know without a doubt unless God moved, there was no way that I would be able to endure this gluten-free journey. If this was clearly from Him, then I wanted Him to make it known and so He did. So be careful what you ask for! So, here I found myself at another pivotal moment.

The shocking moment, while eating a little chicken salad!

In the very first week of this gluten-free journey, there was one day when I sat down at the table to eat some of my favorite chicken salad. I felt like I had been stripped of everything else I loved to eat. As I was preparing my simple plate that only required a fork, I was just desperately wishing and wanting a piece of toasted bread or at least some crackers. I was just a week into this and thought the world had come to an end. So, I thought I would look up the ingredients in the little filo shells that I loved to eat with my chicken salad. Just as I thought, and not to my surprise, they were made of wheat! Wishful thinking! But there was something else in the ingredients that caught my eye that I haven't ever noticed before- **vital wheat gluten**. Hmm…. That was the first time I had seen vital wheat gluten listed as an ingredient. I began to ponder and wonder why and what made that wheat gluten so vital? I thought to myself. "What else Lord?"

Interestingly enough, the word *vital* in Webster's dictionary means "existing as a manifestation of life." Vital Wheat Gluten has the highest protein and gluten content. Now stay with me because I want you to understand what took place that day at my table just having a little chicken salad and wondering what God was up to. At that time, when I looked up vital wheat gluten, another unusual word I had never seen before- *seitan*- caught my attention. There was just something about the way that word looked; it just didn't look or sound right when I pronounced it. I immediately used the dictionary app on my phone to see what that word meant. I looked up the word *seitan*. OH WOW, I was completely shocked the very first time I pressed the microphone in my dictionary app to listen to the word pronunciation. The word *seitan* was pronounced "SATAN"! I replayed it again- "SATAN"- and again- "SATAN". The loud, shocking sound of that word sent chills all over me as I repeatedly listened to it. I encourage you to do the same, to get the full sound effect. I knew there was something significant that my eyes needed to see, and my ears needed to hear. It felt like it was a big discovery of something hidden, but I knew there was something more. It was a shocking moment, yet I felt that all had not been revealed. Now let's look at *seitan* to discover the hidden facts.

Seitan: say-tan (sei- to be, to become) + (tan- as in **"protein"**) is to become protein; is pronounced "Satan." Seitan is a meat substitute made from wheat gluten. Remember gluten is a protein. The meaning of the word seitan has undergone a gradual evolution. Gluten to Seitan! We have gone from grains to proteins.

Since seitan is so much more versatile and acceptable, it is permeating the market at a faster rate than tofu. One of the most common uses of wheat gluten is in vegetarian products such as the *Morning Star Farms* brand. You will see where this brand led me. Gluten is the main protein of wheat. It is also used for protein instead of meat for vegetarian diets for those who practice Buddhism. I believe that gluten was created specifically for the diet of the Asian culture who no longer wanted to eat meat. In another sense, I wondered if it was created because of their own God, Buddha?

CHAPTER 5:

Roman Goddess Grains

Chapter Five:

Roman Goddess Grains

I will elaborate on what I mentioned, in the previous chapter, about Morning Star brand. As you have read, I went from the field to the lab, to the planets, and stars. This journey took me from the ground to the sky and all in between. I had no idea where all this was going, but it was adventurous, to say the least. During my intensive research, I learned about the *Morning Star* brand for vegetarian diets. I looked up the definition of Morning Star, but little did I know where it was going to lead.

Morning Star: Latin translates "Lucifer" as beauty "morning star", the planet **Venus**, or "light-bringing". Venus is named after the Roman goddess of love. The **ancient name for Venus was Lucifer** which means "light bringer"; one who is seen from Earth. It was thought to be two different stars, the evening star, and the morning star, that appeared at sunset and sunrise. I find it rather interesting to give the name *light- bringing* to Lucifer, the one who hides and operates in darkness. Lucifer is one of his names that is used to deceive the nations.

Isaiah 14:12 (NKJV) *How you are fallen from heaven, O Lucifer, son of the morning! How you are cut down to the ground, You who weakened the nations!*

As I researched the planets, I continued to discover more and more. Venus led to Jupiter and to Ishtar and so on to the Queen of Heaven.

Ceres is the Roman goddess of harvest and agriculture, grain crops, and fertility. **Ceres** was a gift to agriculture to humankind. This Roman goddess had the power to fertilize, multiply, and fructify the plant and animal seed. Her laws and rights protected all activities of the agricultural cycle. "Feriae Sementivae" is a Roman Festival of sowing held in honor of Ceres, the goddess of agriculture and the mother of the earth. Ceres has the main festival of Cerealia. Cerealia is the major festival of ancient Roman religion, celebrated for the grain goddess Ceres. **Hosea 2:8-9, 11.**

Cereal derives its name from the dwarf planet Ceres. Cereal grains are the staple of crops. We have adopted and given title to the Roman Goddess of Grain, Ceres, as what we call- Cereal.

Ishtar was the Babylonian and Assyrian mother goddess. Ishtar, the planet Venus, appeared as the queen of heaven. In the time of Jeremiah, the people would worship the queen. However, the main sky deity was seen as feminine and held the title, **Queen of Heaven.** This title was later applied to the **Virgin Mary.**

After wondering why, I was somewhere out in space and being overwhelmed with learning about stars and planets, I was eager to know where and why God was taking me through this process. I felt I had been on a roller-coaster ride, learning about wheat, gluten, Seiten, stars, planets, and now the queen of heaven! I had to laugh and think to myself I was just eating my chicken salad. Believe me, I wondered how I even got here. But I am not surprised. So, let's look at scripture as I continue to on with the **Queen of Heaven**.

CHAPTER 6:

Sacred Raisin Cakes

Chapter Six:

Sacred Raisin Cakes

Hosea 3:1 NIV- *Love her as the Lord loves the Israelites, though they turned to other gods and love their "sacred raisin cakes.*

I dols, Cakes, and Queens, Oh My! This chapter discusses Pagan practices and idol worship! They turned to other gods and loved their sacred raisin cakes! Raisins were delicacies that represented idolatrous worship. Hosea was the ancient prophet of Israel that warned Israel they were guilty of idol worship. They had forgotten the entire land was a gift from God. In Hosea 2:8-11, God warned them since they didn't acknowledge Him, He would take away His grain and new wine they used for Baal. Did God keep His word and take away the grain that was used for worship to false gods? We also see, in two other passages concerning the cakes, in the book of Jeremiah.

Jeremiah 7:18 (NIV)-*The children gather wood, fathers light the fire, and the women knead the dough and make cakes of bread for the queen of heaven.*

Jeremiah 44:19 (NIV)- *We burned incense to the queen of heaven and poured out drink offerings to her; did not our husbands know that we were **making cakes like in her image** and pouring drink offerings to her? But ever since we stopped burning incense to the queen of heaven and pouring out drink to her, we have had nothing and have been perishing by sword and famine.*

Whose image, what queen, and why cakes?

In the time of Jeremiah, the people would worship the queen. Was it for the queen of Jezebel, during the time of King Ahab, who worshiped Baal? In the previous chapter, I had mentioned that the main sky deity was seen as feminine and held the title **Queen of Heaven.** The *raisins cakes* were used for women's Eucharist and religious rituals. The cakes were molded in the form of a female goddess. They were making cakes, in the Queen's image, for pagan worship. They were used for cultic offerings.

Regardless of the opinions of who is clearly defined as the Queen of Heaven, we see that it was not made in the image of the living God, nor for His worship. The ancient cakes, used for the queen, are now modern wafers for the King! If God took away His grain, then what are we offering to Him as we participate in Communion? The same cake that was offered to the false gods of Baal is a counterfeit and imitation of a wafer to the Lord's Supper. The sacred raisin cakes, of idol worship, in the Old Testament, were as vital to the religious practices of the Israelites as our communion is to us. The script has been flipped from sacred raisin cakes for idol worship, to dead false gods, now to false wafers offered to a true living Holy God. Are we playing patty-cake with the devil? *Patty Cake... Patty Cake...Satan's plan... just smooth this over and offer them again!* The idol worship passed on as a ritual of what we call tradition.

CHAPTER 7:

A Seat at His Table!

Chapter Seven:

A Seat at His Table!

Let me remind you that I was in pursuit of God and on an adventurous journey. It was also during this same time that my husband and I were faced with a crisis. He was suddenly going into kidney failure and was in desperate need of a kidney transplant. After learning that devastating news, I felt led to partake daily in Communion, as a couple. As we began the communion journey, I camped out in the Upper Room where it all began.

During this journey of praying, and fasting, I was partaking of communion wafers every day, for every meal. I was believing in a miracle for my husband. I was in constant pursuit and sought after God for answers to my questions and my prayers. The daily partaking in communion led me to "a deeper desire to know Him more intimately". I was eating wafers, like candy, and believing for a miracle!

The Last Supper experience intrigued me on a greater level. It grabbed my attention and curiosity and I couldn't get away from it. I had a strong desire to learn what really took place that day, in The Upper Room. I pray that, as you read this, you will prepare yourself to come along with me, as we enter The Guest Room. One day, I was sitting in my closet praying, reading the Word, and breaking bread. Then suddenly, I felt as if I was sitting at the table with Jesus! The feeling was so surreal. I felt as if I had pulled up a chair at His table and was watching it all take place.

What happened at the table in the Upper Room? Let me tell you what happened and what He revealed to me in His Word. Just like with the disciples, God was also made known to me, in the breaking of the bread.

Luke 24:30 NKJV- *Now it came to pass, as He sat at the table with them, that He took bread, blessed and broke it, and gave it to them. Then their eyes were opened, and they knew Him; and He vanished from their sight.* This reminded me of the day when the Lord spoke to me, saying, *"I will pull the wool and the scales from your eyes."* Just like the disciples, that was when my spiritual eyes were opened and I knew Him.

Just as He revealed Himself to the disciples, He revealed Himself to me, as I sat at the table to learn more about what took place in the Upper Room. It was then that I encountered the presence of God, sitting in my closet in the natural, but at His table in the spirit.

He broke bread, going to the cross, and broke bread after He was resurrected. Just as the disciples' hearts burned, so did mine. In my closet, God opened the Scriptures to me, just as He did for the disciples. Now, He began to shake things up, as I read the words of Jesus in **John 6:53-** *Jesus says, "very truly I tell you, unless you eat the flesh of the Son of Man and drink his blood, you have no life in you.* I thought, for a moment, *"What is He even talking about?"* Then, He reminded me Jesus took on flesh and that the Word became flesh.

His command, to his disciples, at The Lord's Supper in the Upper Room, was **"Do this in remembrance of Me"** ...simply put, let this be the reminder of what I did for you! It was, at that moment, that I had a deep personal revelation of the cost of the cross. I was worth dying for!

Jesus was getting ready to go to the cross to be crucified and His disciples sat arguing and disputing among themselves, all while Judas knew what He was going to do. The Upper Room was the setting He chose to demonstrate his Holy Communion and establish the New Covenant. This was at this time that Jesus shared His last meal with His disciples. Jesus knew that it was important to make His disciples aware of His imminent betrayal and crucifixion. In **John 13:7,** Jesus replied, *"You do not realize what I am doing, but later you will understand."* Jesus was teaching me and them true communion with the Holy Spirit. He was going to the cross and will transition from the flesh to the Spirit.

Their eyes were on themselves and, because of fear, they missed the words of His command. The disciples' inattentiveness and lack of understanding caused them to miss the point of not only what Jesus was saying, but also what He was doing and the significance of this event. The disciples clearly missed the mark on something of such importance. I came to this place, in scripture, that stirred up so many questions in my mind that I wanted to know the answer. It left me wondering and full of questions that sent me on yet another adventurous journey to discover the answer and to gain an understanding. Can you imagine what they must have felt? The fear and anxiety while sitting there not knowing who among them would betray Him? Think about it for a minute. What if today you were faced with those words? Ask yourself, are you a Judas to Jesus? Are you unknowingly denying and betraying Him? I really wanted to know more about the betrayal of Judas.

*And He took bread, gave thanks and broke it, and gave it to them, saying, "This is my body given for you; do this in remembrance of Me. In the same way, **after** supper, He took the cup, saying "This cup is the new covenant in My blood, which is poured out for you."* **Luke 22: 19-20**

The word **after** leaped off the page like never before. I could hear the loud whisper: **"AFTER!"** As I read back over the scriptures, there was a new revelation; something I had never noticed before. There was an emphasis on the word **after.** It was **after** the supper when Jesus took the cup. It was then, **after** the supper, that God put the new covenant into place. Jesus took the cup, but Satan took the bread. Satan wanted to be a part of God's plan and institution of the blood covenant. Satan was only allowed to do what he was assigned to do and nothing more. We know God would not make a covenant with Satan. I will share with you what Satan was assigned to do in the next few chapters.

I sat in my closet, holding wafers in my hand and desiring to know more about that day in the Upper Room. It was there, in my prayer room, that I encountered His presence and my eyes and heart were open.

CHAPTER 8:

The Sifting and the Secret Place

Chapter Eight:

The Sifting and the Secret Place

O ne day, I was in the prayer room at church, and I looked down at this scripture opened in front of me in big flashing words **Luke 22:31-32 (NIV)-** *"Simon, Simon, Satan has asked to sift all of you as wheat. But I have prayed for you, Simon, that your faith may not fail. And when you have turned back, strengthen your brothers."* When the Lord calls your name twice, you better listen! Can you imagine what Simon Peter must have felt at that moment? Notice it was not just Simon to be sifted, He said all of you. Really, out of all the scriptures, this was the one that appeared in front of me as I was praying about my wheat/gluten journey! I didn't understand the importance of those scriptures then, but I sure found out later what they really meant to me personally.

Luke 8:17 (NKJV)- *For nothing is secret that will not be revealed, nor anything hidden that will not be known and come to light.*

At the beginning of the story, I mentioned I felt as if I had a secret. I discovered what that meant. Now I want to show you what I learned about that. Let's take a closer look at the definition of secret.

Secret: not known or seen by others; a mystery.

Latin form is "secretus"; meaning separate, to set apart.

It is from the verb- secernere. Se- "apart" and Cernere- "sift".

I knew the word **sieve** was like sifting, but I never knew the word *secret* had anything to do with sifting.

I was so sifted just like Peter! I still wondered why the reference was to *sift as wheat* and not something else. Out of all the words to be used and at the very moment I was praying about wheat, gluten. It brought forth the question- "Has the wheat been sifted?" Might I ask, was there a secret sifting of the wheat we didn't know about? Remember in Matthew when the enemy came in the night? After all, I had been learning and writing about wheat, this scripture excited me and scared me at the same time. I questioned why, out of all the words in the world, he had used the word *wheat*. Why did Satan use the words- *sift as wheat?* Has the secret of the sifting of the wheat become a great mystery?

Why couldn't he sift him as something else? You know there was a reason Satan asked to sift Peter. During my spiritual journey, I realized that just as Satan did Peter, Satan was going to sift me. I actually put my name in the place of Simon. Instead of Simon, Simon, I read it as *Teresa, Teresa,*

Satan asked to sift you as wheat. I was warned, so I knew growing closer to God would create an attack from Satan, and oh, it surely came! In the midst of the sifting, while writing this book, I was sifted to the core!

As I sought after God, the enemy was in hot pursuit of me. I experienced spiritual warfare, like never before. I encountered a demonic attack, from the pit of Hell. It was confirmed, one night when I heard the words from Dr. Traci Holloman, who prayed over me: *"You know exactly what the Lord has given you"* and *"Satan and his demons come to take you out!"*

The enemy had a plan and plot to try to steal the Word of the Lord and muzzle me. I had a powerful, consuming shift. As a result, I failed and turned my back and ran from God, and went the other way. But what was so very personal and powerful was to read that Jesus said, *"BUT, I have prayed for you, Simon, your faith may not fail, And when you turn back,* not if but when you do, *strengthen your brothers."* I went through the sifting that nearly destroyed me. I experienced the full effect of **James 1:15 (NIV)- ** *"...when sin is full-grown, gives birth to death."* It was from the death that I experienced the redeeming resurrection power of Christ in my life. Satan had a plot, but God had a plan. I was reminded of the same thing He told Peter in **Luke 22:32**: *But I have prayed for you, Simon, that your faith may not fail. And when you have turned back, strengthen your brothers.* The words of Jesus, *"but I have prayed for you,"* went deep into my spirit! I turned back to God because Jesus prayed for me and interceded on my behalf.

It was in the breaking, not only of the bread BUT in my breaking process; it was in the breaking of me!!! It was when I turned back to God that my eyes were opened, and my heart began to burn for Him. He was revealed to me, in the depths of my spirit, just like He was revealed to the disciples on the road to Emmaus. Now, let's look a little deeper in scripture and what really took place at the table during the Supper.

CHAPTER 9:

The Invited Guest and the Unwanted Visitor

Chapter Nine:

The Invited Guest and the Unwanted Visitor

During this time in my life, I was embracing the gift of Holy Communion. I was also in the middle of a chase to find the answer to which wafer I should use in my gluten-free journey. At one point, I was sitting in a hotel room reading a passage in the book of 2 Corinthians and was amazed to see a strangely familiar language there that I had just studied relating to communion. The words- *common, harmony, and fellowship* were almost identical in meaning to those I had studied just prior to reading these verses!

2 Corinthians 6:14-16 (NIV)- *Do not be yoked together with unbelievers. For what do righteousness and wickedness have in* __common__? *Or what* __fellowship__ *can light have with darkness? What* __harmony__ *is there between Christ and Belial? Or what does a believer have in common with an unbeliever? What agreement is there between the temple of God and idols? For we are the temple of the living God.*

So, I looked up the definition of Holy Communion and this is what caught my attention. Let me break this down for you, so you can understand the title of this chapter.

Holy: sacred, consecrated, set apart.

Communion: intimate relationship or rapport, from the Latin for sharing-in **common.**

Holy Communion: 1. the act of receiving the Eucharist elements, 2. fellowship.

Fellowship: companionship, company. As I read the definition of the word- *company,* I noticed that it included the explanation, "associates, visitors, guests, **having a guest for dinner.**"

That's it, and I jumped up! I thought about The Upper Room and that Judas was the invited guest, but Satan was the unwanted visitor. So, let's look at the visitation from the visitor.

I was diligently studying God's word and came to a place in scripture that I just couldn't leave. I found it quite interesting, and it captured my full attention. Throughout my reading of the Bible, I don't think anything has ever caught my curiosity quite like this. What in the world even took place during that moment that happened so quickly? Something so important happened within the blink of an eye. It was the most built-up anticipation I have ever had as I continued to read on to see what really happened.

When the enemy comes in to rob the house they come quickly and with an agenda. They do not need your house keys or an invitation to intrude. Thieves don't come to linger; they will always have the quickest drive-by visits and quickly steal what they come for. It was very evident that Satan got in the Upper Room. We can see where two passages read that Satan entered Judas twice. First, when he agreed to hand Jesus over in exchange for thirty pieces of silver. Did Satan use Judas to buy his way into the supper? We think Judas sold Jesus, but he did not sell Jesus; in actuality, poor Judas sold his very own soul! The exchange was not only of money but of his salvation.

Now, let's consider the second exchange at the table during the Lord's Supper. You can see where Satan entered Judas the second time. At that point was Jesus speaking to Judas or Satan? Why would Jesus invite Judas and speak those words? Jesus was speaking directly to Satan through Judas. Jesus literally meant what He said when He spoke, **"Do what you come to do and do it quickly."** In other words, get it and get out! Hold on a moment! But what did He come to do? We see the urgency of the timing, for the fact that Satan cannot stand in the midst of Jesus. Judas, in flesh, took the bread, went out, and it was night! Where was Satan? Where is the bread? What is that bread? What did you do with that bread if you went all the way to the upper room to get it? Did he leave with Judas? Did he leave with the bread? Where is that bread at? Wait, what just happened? This happened way too fast; in a blink of an eye. I just felt like I ran out of the room chasing Judas and hollering what are you doing? Bring that bread back! I felt like I was in an action movie. But it was no longer Judas; it was Satan who had taken over and led Judas right to the tree to commit suicide by hanging himself.

The enemy operates in secret and in the darkness. So, what happened afterward? Just like that and it's over? Did something happen beyond the spiritual realm that we cannot see in the natural? I found myself so caught up in this passage that I stayed in the closet reading and praying for days upon days.

Did Satan really want us to break bread in remembrance of him without us even knowing it?

I began to call out, "Tell me more Lord, I wanna know more, I gotta know more. Lord, I wanna know exactly what took place." The questions began, "What did he come to do so quickly and why was it all over just like that?" That was the quickest drive-by visit I had ever seen. Surely there had to have been a hidden agenda going on. As if betraying Him with a kiss in the garden wasn't enough, Satan went all the way to the Upper Room the night before Jesus was crucified. It is safe to say the enemy got in. We know evil practices don't just go away; they evolve. This made me eager to learn what really took place and why Satan would have even been allowed in The Upper Room. **Only God could allow permission for the visitation!**

The next part of this scripture passage came with flashing red lights and leaped off the page. **John 13:30 (NIV)-** *As soon as Judas had taken the bread, he went out. And it was night.* Immediately, after reading this, my thoughts led me straight to this scripture in Matthew 13. This place in scripture was like watching an action movie and you were waiting with such suspense to see what happened, and suddenly, just like that, it ended with... *To be continued*... What! **And it was Night....**

John 13:27-30 (NIV)- *As soon as Judas took the bread, Satan entered into him. So Jesus told him, "What you are about to do, do quickly."* But **no one** at the meal understood why Jesus said this to him. Since Judas had charge of the money, some thought Jesus was telling him to buy what was needed for the festival or to give something to the poor. **As soon as Judas had taken the bread, he went out. And it was night.**

Jesus didn't ask- "What are you about to do?" He said- "What you are about to do." He knew exactly what was going to take place. I can't even imagine sitting at the table with Jesus as He spoke, *"one of you will betray me"*. Just what if the very moment we betrayed Jesus, Satan entered us? Think about that for a moment and read that again out loud!

As soon as I read that passage my mind went right back to the *Parable of the Wheat* in the book of Matthew. **Matthew 13:24 (NIV)** *The kingdom of heaven is like a man who sowed good seeds in his field.* **But while everyone was sleeping,** *the enemy came and sowed weeds among the wheat, and went away.* The enemy came and sowed among the wheat that we eat, while we were all napping.

This is the passage that plays over and over in my mind. I could just envision this whole scene during the meal. The disciples sat and argued about who was going to betray him and clearly did not even see what was taking place around them. Why did all this take place if it was not of importance or God's will? I asked about Judas and what the matter of taking the bread was. Was Judas **taking or partaking**? In what matter was the retrieval of the bread? Also, was Satan through Judas, allowed to partake in the Lord's Supper or was he trying to **gain possession**? To take or to partake?

Partake: to take part in or experience something along with others.

Take: To get into one's possession or hand; **to control,** to seize, to capture. Took, take, taken; a verb to show action.

As soon as Judas received the bread, Satan simultaneously entered him at that very moment. Who was Jesus talking to at the moment? Was He speaking directly to Satan through Judas? Satan wanted to take control to gain power. If I had to guess, Satan had a bigger agenda that we can't see with the physical eye. No one understood why Jesus said this to him. In the physical it was Judas, but in the spiritual it was Satan! During that time, the disciples stared at one another, at a loss to know what Jesus meant. Simon Peter then motioned to John and said, "*Ask Him which one is He referring to.*" That is the very same question I was asking, "*Who are you referring to*"? The disciples were more concerned with which one was going to betray Him than what was being done.

If Satan got into the Lord's supper, do you believe he made his way into the church in the communion wafer that we partake of today? The scheme of Satan would be to have us dishonor God without even being aware of our transgression. Not only did the betrayal take place during the Lord's Supper but continued through the sacrament of partaking of the wafer, as well.

The enemy with his craftiness loves to destroy us in any way possible. What was meant for our health, the enemy distorted and used against us. As in communion, he made a mockery out of God. **There will always be a counterfeit for the real thing.** I will expose another secret plot of the counterfeit in this next chapter.

CHAPTER 10:

Watch Out For That Wafer!

Chapter Ten:

Watch Out for that Wafer!

I f I had to put this book in the chronological order of events, this chapter would be close to first. The title of this chapter was the exact words Mama Claire spoke to me on that day. That particular weekend, we went to Charlotte to visit David's parents, whom I respectfully acknowledge as being instrumental in this journey. My mother-in-love, whom we call Mama Claire, has a sweet gentle spirit, is always so kind and friendly to every person, and has never met a stranger. I am not kidding when I say every restaurant we visited, knew her by name and knew her order. As she would introduce us and explain this gluten thing to others, I can honestly say, every single time, without hesitation, she would always say the very same words to them, "We passed down our genes." And every time, I thought to myself, "Are these good genes or bad genes? Needless to say, in the beginning, I was not very happy with this change! I did not like it; I did not agree with it, and I certainly did not want to embrace it. But I did!

Let me tell you about the very next day during lunch. Mama Claire spoke something that I did not grasp in the moment. However, later as I sought after God, He brought me back to my remembrance that very day, sitting at the table with her and hearing those words that she spoke to me. These powerful words from her mouth, *"Watch Out for That Wafer,"* *became* the very title of this chapter.

I was reminded of the words that Mama Claire spoke to me: "Watch out for that wafer!" It never even registered with me, at that time, the power of those words and what they really meant. At that moment, I didn't really care about a communion wafer, and even thought to myself, "Why is she telling me this?" I just wanted to eat my gluten food. I was more worried about what my family was going to eat on a daily basis than occasionally taking a wafer and participating in communion. What I did not realize was that Mama Claire used the very same words Jesus spoke in Matthew, I was shocked to read it again in **Matthew 16:6** *"Watch out!" Jesus warned them. "Beware of the yeast of the Pharisees and Sadducees."* You have been warned!

This chapter took place at the beginning of my gluten-free life-changing journey, shortly after my surprise chicken salad lunch. But that day quickly came, and I was faced with a dilemma and a decision that was far greater than I could even begin to think or imagine: The Communion Wafer! Oh, my Lord, what am I to do? I remember that intense moment when I was faced with Communion for the very first time since becoming gluten-free. Those soft-spoken words came back in a silent whisper from Mama Claire,

"Watch out for that wafer!" Those words loudly echoed all the way back from Charlotte, North Carolina.

After becoming gluten-free and adapting to the lifestyle, I knew there was more to be known. Yet, little did I know, the answer I was looking and waiting for was right among me. The moment came when I was faced with Communion and the receiving of the gluten wafer. As I stood facing the Communion tray, I slammed on the brakes in a slow-motion movement. There I stood like a deer frozen in the blinding glare of headlights, or a squirrel in the middle of the road trying to decide which way to run. I felt I needed an immediate response from God. I didn't know what to do! I returned to my seat after proceeding through the line empty-handed and I began to weep and cry out, "Oh God! What should I do???" I did not want to avoid taking the wafer, but at that very moment, I was not sure what to do. I earnestly prayed and asked another huge and important question that would change everything that I was taught, and that was a scary thought. I was nervous; I was scared and perplexed. I didn't want to be different, I wanted to be like everyone else. I said to myself, "I mean really, it's not gonna kill me. So just take it, it would be a simple solution and quick fix." But I stopped and asked this provoking question:

"God, if it is Your will for my life to be gluten-free, then should I be taking this wheat gluten-filled wafer?"

My head was spinning and filled with so many thoughts: "Oh God, I cry out to you! **Am I taking the right wafer?** Am I being too spiritual? Am I being too liberal? Am I religious or legalistic? Is this from you? What am I to do? Help me! I have taken the same wafer, for thirty-five years, why should I change now? I just didn't take this very lightly or half-heartedly.

Later, I even asked myself, "Why do I even partake of the wafer? It's just a wafer- surely, it's okay? Questions upon questions, flooded my mind. I began to cry with a voice of desperation. "Oh God help me!" Please talk to me about this wafer! I need You to answer me.

I had been long seeking His perfect will, His plan, and purpose for my life. I truly desired to be in the center of His will. I don't know if I could truly express to you the overwhelming sense of fear, doubt, worry, and every emotion possible that consumed me. But His Holy Spirit brought peace to me while seeking truth. I was afraid to make the change with the wafers because it was all I ever knew. I remember standing in the midst of the congregation silently crying out in desperation. "Why God? Why Me?" I can honestly say, the struggle was very much real. I thought back and remembered the sound of *seitan* and how we were using a wafer with wheat gluten in it that is genetically modified and originated from and for Buddhism. I thought of the scripture passage of the sacred raisin cakes that were made for the queen of heaven. What queen? Jezebel, Mary? I thought about so many different things. I thought about the parable of the wheat and what the enemy did while we were sleeping. Is it too early in the story to ask a very simple question: have we brought the sacred raisin cakes that were made into the image of the queen of heaven to the Lord's Supper to *Do in Remembrance of Him?*

Well, if one time wasn't enough, there was a second time and third time I was faced with communion before I knew what to do about the wafer. I really took this decision to heart and was very serious about seeking God for the right answer to this wafer-taking issue. I just wanted to go back to my old ways and eat my gluten and not have to worry about taking which wafer so everything would be okay. Once again, I was not concerned with the medical aspect of receiving the wafer because it was not like a life-or-death situation. I mean, it is just a wafer right; well, not for me! It was much more than that. I was more concerned with what God wanted me to do. **Honestly, it would have been a whole lot easier to just go right through that line and take that wafer and hush my mouth. But, nope, not me! Just keep walking Teresa!**

I honestly felt I was wrestling between flesh and spirit in those moments. Then there was the third time I was unexpectedly faced with communion. I just walked out of service as it was taking place. I went out and I cried, and I prayed. I still did not have the answer to my question. I didn't feel the need or have peace about receiving the wafer. I still needed an answer with what to do about this Communion wafer. This seemed like yet another whole journey in itself! I knew God had delivered me from gluten and it was His will for my life. I began to ask about Communion and His will concerning which wafer to use. I just thought it was contradictory to live a gluten-free lifestyle and go take a wafer that is gluten. I thought the diet change was a real struggle, but not nearly like the change of the wafer. Wow, that's it! The whole reason for this gluten-free journey. **I didn't know, at the time, that the change in my lifestyle would bring about a change of the wafer.** It was much easier to just take the same wafer and let it be. I desired the answer from God and wanted confirmation as to what to do with this decision I was faced with. *Watch out for the wafer* led to *watch out and be on guard against the traditions.*

CHAPTER 11:

Religious Traditions of Man

Chapter Eleven:

Religious Traditions of Man

A s time passed, I began to hear God speak to me about **traditions**. I wasn't exactly sure what that meant at the time, because we were nearing the holidays. I just waited for God to teach me what He wanted me to know about **traditions** and of course, He took me to His Word.

Mark 7: 3-9; 13 *The Pharisees and Jews don't eat unless they give their hands a ceremonial washing holding on to their traditions of the elders.4 When they come to the marketplace, they do not eat unless they wash. They observe many other traditions. 5 So the Pharisees and teachers of the Law asked Jesus, "Why don't your disciples live according to the traditions of the elders instead of eating their food with unclean hands?" 6 He replied, "Isaiah was right when he prophesied about you hypocrites; as it is written: These people honor me with their lips, but their hearts are far from me. 7 They worship me in vain; their teachings are merely human rules. 8 You have let go of the commands of God and are holding on to human traditions of men. 9 You have a fine way of setting aside the commands of God in order to observe your own traditions, 13 thus you nullify the word of God by your tradition that you have handed down.*

What **tradition** has been handed down? What have we adopted that was not meant to be adopted? I began to think about the scripture and wondered what in the world does this all mean. I questioned: "What **traditions** have been handed down through the church?" Not just in our lives, but as the body of Christ. Because of traditions, you made the Word of God no effect. And then, another scripture passage came to me, and it was like popcorn popping all throughout His words.

So, let's look at the definition.

Tradition- related to a tradition: handed down from age to age; following or conforming to tradition: adhering to past practices.

Colossians 2:8- *See to it that no one takes you captive through hollow and deceptive philosophy, which depends on <u>human tradition</u> and the basic principles of this world, rather than Christ.*

Matthew 16:11-12- *Pharisees and Sadducees How is it you don't understand that I'm not talking to you about bread.* **Be on guard against the yeast** *of the Pharisees and Sadducees. Then they understood that He was not telling them to guard against the yeast used in bread,* **but against the teaching** *of the Pharisees and Sadducees.*

Matthew 16:12 (MSG)- *Haven't you realized yet that bread isn't the problem? The problem is yeast, Pharisee- Sadducees yeast. Then they got it, that He wasn't concerned* **about eating, but teaching.**

Would changing wafers change the tradition? If you change the tradition, will it change the teaching?

Then I learned that the Passover Meal was the festival of **unleavened** bread! They were to save a little of the dough as a starter for the next batch. Well, this sent me to Matthew 13:33 and the parable of the kingdom and yeast. How fast can something permeate and what has permeated? I spent time meditating on this scripture and asking God for understanding. What does this mean and how does the parable apply? What has been done and what have we been taught? What teaching should we be on guard against as you say in your word? All I could say was, *teach me, Lord.*

CHAPTER 12:

Living in the Shadows

Chapter Twelve:

Living in the Shadows

Shadows are a reflected image and area of darkness created when a source of light is blocked.

The big shadow is a mere reflection of things from the past projecting forward. Are we living in the darkness from the shadows that we are facing? God is removing the source that blocks the light. This led to this question: **I often wondered if we have been living in the shadows of the Roman Catholics over the past decades?**

Colossians 2:16-17- *So let no one judge you in food or in drink, or regarding a festival or a new moon or sabbaths, which are a shadow of things to come, but the substance is of Christ.*

I question whether this is a matter that has not been brought to light since the beginning of the Reformation. I never thought when I began my gluten-free journey that I would end up here. The Catholic Church adopted the following scripture because Jesus likened himself to wheat before His crucifixion: ***John 12:24-*** *Very truly I tell you the truth; unless a* *kernel of wheat falls to the ground and dies it remains a single seed, but if it dies, it produces many seeds.*

I began wondering- Did Jesus see himself as a kernel of wheat, or was He using a metaphor; another parable to tell the story? **Did this scripture validate the Catholic doctrine of what substance the communion wafer should be made of?** Definitely not a genetically modified, glutenized wafer! This led me to the Code of Canon and the Reformation.

If we are the reformed, then why are we still hiding in the shadows and living under the Catholic law? What is done in the dark will always come to light! We see in different text about what is hidden shall be revealed and what is in darkness shall be brought to light. We are to come out and be separate. One thing I know for sure is religion must die so that you may live freely in the resurrection power of Jesus Christ.

If the Catholic law demands that gluten has to be in the wafer, I will stand against them and say, *NO it does not have to be!*

The hour of Reformation has come!

CHAPTER 13:

Cracking the Code

Chapter Thirteen:

Cracking the Code

The Code of Canon Law is the book of Catholic law. In my search, I discovered that the communion wafer must be made from wheat. I stumbled across this fact that I was unaware of and found it to be very interesting. I did not grow up in the Catholic faith, so I was not familiar with The Code of Canon Law. The Canon Law is a body of laws and regulations made or adopted by ecclesiastical authority. It is the internal law governing the Catholic Church. A doctrine of demons? I was in complete shock and very much surprised by the information about The Holy Communion in the book, The Code of Canon Law. Code of Canon 924.2 states- "The bread must be only made with wheat" Shortly after this discovery, I received from my former Catholic friend, the newest revised version of The Code of Canon Law. I was astonished that in the new revised version, the word "wheat" had changed to "gluten!" Code of Canon 924.2, now says that **"bread without any "gluten" is invalid matter, by which the wafer without gluten now is invalid."** I find it interesting that gluten is a required matter for the Communion wafer to be validated for the host. Catholics believe that the Communion wafer should be made of wheat, since in the newest revised version, it now is recorded as gluten. How interesting is that?

Their **tradition** will not accept a gluten-free wafer, for it has to contain .0001%, the lowest amount of gluten possible to keep the wheat in the wafer because the gluten is in the wheat. This moment changed everything for me. From the short time of finding the initial information to receiving the new book as a gift, the code had already been revised to read gluten instead of wheat. I will strongly say that a wafer that has gluten should NOT be a valid matter. This one line just defended every word I have spoken concerning what wafer to use for Communion. We need to know where things originated from and why there are such legalistic, religious requirements.

So, I must ask the question, **"Did the canon misfire?"** Why does the Catholic Church feel so strongly about glutenized wafers?

Colossians 2:14-15- *Having canceled the **written code** with its regulations, that was against us and that stood opposed to us, He took it away, nailing it to the cross. And having disarmed the powers and authorities, He made a public spectacle of them, triumphing over them by the cross.*

The Sacraments are integral to Catholic liturgical worship. The principal Sacrament is the Eucharist, also known as the Mass. Sadly, it is a mass of a crowd being led in the wrong direction. The Catholics teach that in this Sacrament, the bread and the wine consecrated only by the priest become the body and blood of Christ. When I learned this, I was blown away and taken aback by such deception. The change that takes place is known as *transubstantiation*. The word *metousiosis* in Greek is "to change" and to "transfer."

Transubstantiation- Catholic Belief

1. An act or instance of transubstantiation, being changed from one **substance** to another **2.** The miraculous change by which, according to Roman Catholic and Eastern Orthodox dogma, the Eucharistic elements at their consecration become the body and blood of Christ while keeping only the appearance of bread and wine. The process by which the bread and wine of the Eucharist is transformed into the body and blood of Jesus Christ. Catholics believe that through transubstantiation the risen Jesus becomes truly present in the Eucharist.

A transfer takes place which is a change, an exchange, a switch.

Trans- across, beyond, through. Some kind of change has taken place

Substantiation- substance, a thing's deepest being, what it is, and of itself, but doesn't capture what is in the substance. In transubstantiation, the bread and wine change into the body and blood of Jesus Christ. Roman Catholic theology holds the doctrine that in the Eucharist, the substance of the bread and the wine used in the Sacrament is changed into the substance of the body and blood of Jesus. If anybody could really believe or think that an actual wafer transforms into the body of Christ, he or she has been bewitched. Sadly, but truly, that would constitute a form of witchcraft.

Consubstantiation- Christian Belief

This is the view that the elements of bread and wine remain the same, while the spirit of God is with the bread and wine. The Catholics put great emphasis on the ingredients of the wafer and the priest during Holy Communion. The following scripture spoke volumes about this teaching of transubstantiation.

Colossians 2:5 (NIV)- *For though I am absent from you in body, I am present with you in spirit and delight to see how orderly you are and how firm your faith in Christ is.*

Colossians 20-23- *Since you died with Christ to the elemental spiritual forces of this world, why, as though you still belonged to the world, do you submit to its rules: "Do not handle! Do not taste! Do not touch!" These rules, which have to do with things that are all destined to perish with use, are based on merely human commands and teachings. Such regulations indeed have an appearance of wisdom, with their self-imposed worship, their false humility, and their harsh treatment of the body, but they lack any value in restraining sensual indulgence.*

The phrase, **"Do not handle! Do not taste! Do not touch it!"** This reminded me of how the priest places the wafer into congregants' mouths during Communion. What has been a question from the beginning of my journey yet remains. Should we be using the same wafer as the Roman Catholics for Communion? I raise the question-If the Roman Catholics got the teachings wrong that Martin Luther protested in his *Ninety-five*

Theses of 1517; did they also get the kind of wafer wrong? This is a continuation of the protest. From the Diet of Worms to the Diet of the Wafers!

CHAPTER 14:

Wearing the Divorce Wedding Band

Chapter Fourteen:

Wearing the Divorce Wedding Band

I was on the journey, a long time, before I received the answer I had been praying for. I was wanting something to be able to use as a metaphor, the right example that could tie this all together. I needed His help to deliver what I was trying to say and to find the right way to communicate this concept. I prayed for God to help me and give me an analogy, and allegory to best describe the wafer and separation from the Catholics. After many prayers, He dropped this in my spirit. The symbolic representation of marriage is with the joining of the rings. If a couple decides to divorce, they drop the name and typically remove the rings that join them together to signify that they are no longer married or in covenant with one another. I believe that if we have divorced ourselves from the Roman Catholic church that Martin Luther criticized for how they performed communion, we question certain practices. Yes, I believe that our teachings are different and not the same. Therefore, my question is- "Should we use the same wafer as they do for our Communion? If they got the teachings and doctrines wrong, can we trust that the use of the exact same wafer is correct? They now have put in a new demand, law, and order; that the wafer must have gluten to be valid. Why does the Catholic Church feel so strongly about the mandate for the gluten-filled wafer?

If we don't agree with the teaching of the Catholics concerning communion, then how can we be sure and believe and trust that we are using the right wafer? Have we spiritually discerned the teaching about Communion; yet still use the same wafer?

When a couple separates or divorces, there is a removal of rings, and in some cases, women will change back to their maiden name. As we have separated from Catholicism to Protestantism, we changed our name but continued to use the same wafer that the Catholic doctrine and law require. **As rings are symbolic for marriage (covenant), so too is the wafer for communion.** Does the use of the same wafer tie us to the Catholic faith? If we are fully separated, shouldn't we retain and reframe from the use of the same wafer? I must ask the questions: "Are we partially separated, or have we **fully divorced? Are we in a "covenant"? Let me encourage you to take that ring off.** We separated from the Catholics but remained connected by using the same wafer. This makes me question why we hold onto the same wafer, using what the Catholic Code of Canon Law demands, rather than seeking truth from God's Word for ourselves. Is the use of the same wafer a lie to tie us to Catholicism?

Letting go of the wedding band and the changing of the name is an obvious analogy that represents the hour of Reformation. I went to a weekend revival at the Ark Fellowship looking for a word from the Lord, especially related to my book. Brian Williams quoted, "There is a desperate need for reformation. God always finds a man or woman that He can entrust the mysteries of heaven to". I felt I was that woman, who God found, that He could trust with the kingdom assignment!

If we are cutting ties, and being reformed, shouldn't we have let go of the same wafer? Also, should we continue to take a wafer that is mandated by the laws of the Catholic Church? Martin Luther himself asked not to be called a Lutheran but rather a Christian. Luther clearly made it known that the teachings he professed, were not of his own, but rather of Christ, for he was not crucified for anyone. We as Christians took on the name Protestants, from the Reformation, but what all was reformed? In the 16th century, the Reformation was a movement that posed a challenge from Martin Luther to the Roman Catholic Church. I may not have a *Ninety-five Theses* statement, but what I do have is an awakening and a divine revelation from the Lord!

According to the Catholic belief, to some Mary is held in higher esteem than Jesus because Mary gave birth to Jesus. The title may have been given to the Queen of Heaven or to Mary, but the status and position belong to Christ.

God created heaven and earth. God made man in his own image. God existed before Mary. Mary is the birth mother of Jesus, but not the "God-bearer." Jesus is the Son of God! God is seen in the three persons in one: God the Father, the Son, and the Holy Spirit. Nowhere is Mary ever found as a member of the Trinity nor does it say "Mary, Mother of God," "Our Lady of Guadalupe", or **"Queen of Heaven."** Catholics worship and idolize Mary as their god.

The **Queen of Heaven** is the title given to the "blessed Virgin Mary," mainly within the Roman Catholic Church. **Have we brought those sacred raisin cakes that were made into the image of the queen of heaven to the Lord's Supper to "Do in Remembrance of Him"?** This last realization leads directly to a new and powerful understanding.

The communion wafer that we use as Christians is not a grain but a genetically modified protein. It was given the name Seitan but pronounced Satan. Seitan is a flavored Wheat gluten used as a meat substitute for vegetarians; it originated in China and Japan for Buddhism; used by Buddhist monks. Yet, we offer it to our Holy God. We are not offering a grain to Him; we are offering a genetically modified protein to our Holy God that represents the body of Jesus Christ!

He said my people will perish for lack of knowledge. He also said, in His Word, that is why so many of you are sick and have fallen asleep. It said on the night he took bread; he was betrayed. I often wondered why those two words had to be in the same sentence. I believe we have been betrayed. My prayer would be that we seek God for his truth in what we should take for the wafer in Holy Communion. It is not my desire to judge, or convict, for that is the work of the Holy Spirit. My sole purpose is to gently share my journey and shed light on what is buried in darkness. I do believe anything outside of God's plan or will is simply from man. I don't feel we should take lightly the command He has given us the night before He was crucified. Anything that is done with abuse is blasphemy and sacrilege. I would have to ask the question: "Are we showing true respect as we participate in Communion?"

Blasphemy: great disrespect shown to God or to something holy; something said or done that is disrespectful to God or to something holy.

Sacrilege: an act of treating a holy place or object in a way that does not show proper respect.

The Catholics believe in Jesus, but their belief and worship are in Mary the mother of Jesus. In the Old Testament, the sacred raisin cakes were made and used to honor and worship false gods, and now, Mary the Queen of Heaven.

When we separated from Catholics, we changed our name but kept the **tradition** of the same communion wafer. It is **easier to criticize the change and cling to the familiar_than to make a change. The wafer that was made for the queen in the Old Testament, is the same wafer we use today for the King.**

We offer a counterfeit communion wafer to a real, living, Holy God in remembrance of Him.

Counterfeit: is to imitate or feign, especially with intent to deceive; also: to make a fraudulent replica of; to engage in counterfeiting something of value.

Wow, a fraudulent replica!

A wafer originated from Buddhism for vegetarian diets, made of wheat and given the name seitan pronounced "satan," adopted as the Catholic Faith ordered in the Code of Canon. We followed the traditions of the Catholic religion and never questioned the wafer at the time when we walked separated as Protestants. We must stop and ask God the what, the how, the why, and the way we participate in Communion!

Papacy- (PAPA) - Father- Papacy is the system of **government** of the Roman Catholic Church in which the Pope is the head of the Catholic Church, the High Priest to whom others confess, and who can forgive people of their sins. This pure religion of witchcraft is trying to control others. Jesus Christ is the only one that can forgive your sins and the sins of the world. It is not only about the bread in Communion but the wine that represents His blood. The enemy went into the upper room to confiscate the bread but could not come near or not touch the blood of Christ. In Revelation 6:6- He said **do not** *damage the oil and the wine* but does that mean the bread/wheat has been damaged? *The Oil* is His Holy Spirit, and *the Wine* is His Blood!

Breaking the Fear of Man

In the middle of the journey, I began to lose faith and was overtaken and crippled by fear of men's opinions. I could actually understand what Martin Luther must have felt. The torment in my mind was beyond what I could bear. Even in the midst of wanting to quit, give up and throw the towel in, I couldn't. My heart was steadfast, and my purpose was sewn into the depths of my spirit. Martin Luther's story motivated me to have his kind of radical faith. He boldly refused to recant and was known as a heretic. For every call, there is an attack. I know it is true that Satan is after the seed that God plants in us. I believe Satan does not want the plots and schemes to be exposed.

I have experienced spiritual warfare like never before. The agony and despair of wondering if this is even real at all; begging Him, **"Don't let me add to or take away from Your word."** I would call it desperation in despair. For every question of denial, there was the answer of truth. For every question along the way, God had an answer. I realized I was seeking man's approval and was worried about what others would think. I doubted that people would understand or even believe my journey. I told God I trusted Him, but I didn't trust myself, and I couldn't do it on my own strength. These were some of his responses to all my questions, excuses, concerns, fears, and doubts. I remember the day he spoke each one of these directly to my heart.

Corinthians 2:4 (NIV)- *My message and my preaching were not with wise and persuasive words, but with a demonstration of the Spirit's power, so that your faith might not rest on human wisdom but God's power.*

When I began to think I could do it on my own, He reminded me of **Proverbs 28:26 (NIV)-** *Those whose trust in themselves are fools, but those who walk in wisdom are kept safe.*

I was worried about everyone else's opinion and what they would think so He gave me: **Galatians 1:10-12 (NIV)-** *If I were still trying to please men, I would not be a servant of Christ. I did not receive it from any man nor was I taught it, rather I received it by revelation from Jesus Christ.*

I remember saying, "But God, people are gonna think I'm crazy." These are the scriptures I was given:

2 Corinthians 5:13 (NIV)- *If we are "out of our mind" as some say, it is for God; if we are in our right mind, it is for you*

Ezekiel 2:7 (NIV)- *You must speak my words to them, whether they listen or fail to listen.*

At that same revival, Jeremiah Johnson prayed over me that the fear of man would be broken off my life. God broke the unhealthy fear of man and restored to me a healthy fear of God! I was able to just trust and rest in the words of Zechariah. **Zechariah 4:6 (NIV)-** *So he said to me, "This is the word of the Lord to Zerubbabel: 'Not by might nor by power, but by my Spirit,' says the Lord Almighty.*

CHAPTER 15:

Who Do You Say I Am?

Chapter Fifteen:

Who Do You Say I Am?

A s I was trying to process this whole journey, I constantly kept asking many questions. I will never forget that moment when I simply asked, "God what do you say?" Immediately He responded, and so nicely turned the question back to me. "Who do you say I am?" That was another defining moment in my life. At the time I didn't understand the importance and the very depth of that question. Honestly, I had never thought about whether I could confidently answer that question to convince someone else that I knew who God was. Well, I soon found out when I went searching for Him. I wanted to know for myself; not just rely on what I have heard others say. So, I asked myself that very same question, "Who do I say He is? I found out. I began to repeat the words of the disciples. "You are the Christ, the Messiah, the Son of the Living God, The Resurrected King, King of King, Lord of Lord, My Lord and Savior!" and so on. As I continued to declare His identity, something resurrected in my spirit! As I proclaimed His names, the spirit of truth began to set me free!

One day, I was sitting on the couch reading the bible and I was reflecting on the ones that had their names changed by Jesus. I thought that was just a very neat concept and what an honor that must have been. I was telling my husband, David, about it, and how it must have felt walking so close with Jesus that He would change your name. Little did I know that several months later, I would ask God, "Who do say I am?" It was, during a quiet moment, when I began to pray, and I asked God that big question. As I was praying, I said, "You have pruned, crushed, and refined me. You redeemed me, restored me, and delivered me; I am yours. I have been identified, sanctified, and justified. I have been made new. So, I began calling out the names of biblical men and women that God had used. I called out "Abraham, Sara, Simon Peter, Saul, and Paul." I began asking Him, "Who do You say I am? Who am I? What do you call me? If You have called me, redeemed me, identified me, sanctified me, and anointed me, then who am I? I'm not just *Teresa* to you.

God spoke to me and said, "FARRO!" I stopped praying and said, "What did you say? Did I hear you speak to me? Farro?" He replied and spelled it to me, "F-A-R-R-O." I had no idea what that even meant, but I couldn't help but think of "Pharaoh." So, I pulled myself together, wiped my eyes, and began to type in "Farro" to Google to see what it meant. I was completely shocked when it was right before my eyes. A picture of wheat and the caption below caught my eye. This was the picture that was worth *more* than a thousand words. WOW! "God is really talking to me about **wheat,** and you called me by name, according to my purpose." Then, God spoke, *I have summoned you by name.* **Isaiah 43: 1**

The caption under the wheat image was this: *Triticum dicoccum*, **emmer wheat, produces what is sometimes called "true" Farro.** That was a moment that took my breath away. There are no real words I could find to even begin to describe what I felt. He took me back to the book of Matthew again and reminded me that I am the true wheat as a believer in Christ and I belong to Him. I was so overwhelmed with emotions but feasting on the moment. It was later that I began to wonder what "Teresa" meant, so I looked up the meaning and to my surprise, it too, was related to my long journey and the story I was writing!

Teresa means "Harvester, Reaper"

I am the true wheat, and I will reap a harvest. Every time I see "Farro", it reminds me all over again of that day I sat before the Lord and He answered. Another reminder of the importance of one's name occurred one day when I was reading a book about praying circles around your children and discovered this sentence: **"Our true identity will only be revealed on the day our heavenly father calls us by our new name."** The enemy tried to destroy my identity, and now my true identity has been revealed in Jesus Christ alone.

In Summary

In Summary

A true statement is that the journey awaits! I fully surrendered to Him and desired His will, His plan, and His purpose for my life. I remember before I started on this journey, I said these words, "Send me Lord, I will go, I will do whatever you have called me to do." This beginning of my journey started with my willingness to fully surrender to God. It started as a need to learn about a gluten-free diet. Initially, it was a health concern for my family, but led to many spiritual implications that caused me to dig deeper. During that season my husband's health declined and he was in kidney failure. I was so desperate for my husband to receive a kidney; I was willing to give up anything. At least I thought I was ready! At first, as you have read, I had a hard time accepting the gluten-free diet. At the beginning of this gluten-free journey, I thought, "Surely, God, you are not using me to tell somebody else what they should and should not eat. I am not the healthiest person to talk about a certain diet. I am overweight and under-tall, out of shape, and shouldn't tell anybody anything about their diet! You picked the wrong one to do this. Needless to say, there was no negotiating, but boy did I learn a lot of things!

Now, I am not a dietician, a physician, a scientist, an astronomist, or an agronomist. I have no education in these areas. I am a yielded vessel to be used for the glory of God. I had no idea what the next part of this journey would look like. All I knew, at that moment, was that I required God's power to even go one meal gluten-free. I believe that I could never have given up the foods containing wheat/gluten, which is in nearly everything, without help from God. I know there was a supernatural deliverance that took place. In the midst of the sifting taking place and while diligently seeking Him, He showed up once again.

The next part of the journey was much bigger than a change of diet. I was excited and scared all at the same time. I thought embracing the diet change was hard, but the next part of the journey was much greater than that. Suddenly, I found myself walking through the line at church to receive Communion. As I walk through the communion line, everything came flooding back to my remembrance and I heard the words, *Watch Out!* These were the very same words, from Mama Claire, that day, sitting at the table. Surprisingly, I was faced with a decision: whether or not to receive communion, because of it not being a gluten-free wafer. This happened on three separate occasions. I strongly believed after becoming gluten-free and with the spiritual implications, that it was contradictory to take the traditional wafer containing wheat/gluten.

I began to fast and pray for the answer about changing to gluten-free wafers. I didn't know what to do because I had taken the same wafer my whole life. I really wished there was a way to express the agony, the sweat, the tears, the doubts, and fears that came with seeking and yielding to His will. Well, I ordered the gluten-free wafers. The spiritual implications were much greater to me than any other reason. It was much greater than the fear and approval of man. In the beginning, I was so worried about what others would think because of my reason for abstaining from the church's traditional wafers and partaking in something different than others. During the process, I now have a greater desire to take Communion more often rather than just on special occasions. This journey has brought me deeper into God's Word and closer to Him.

I hope people will understand that the last thing Jesus did before he was crucified was to commune with his disciples. He asked us to do this in remembrance of Him, which is a command, not a suggestion.

I did not want to take this command lightly or casually. Often during communion, I imagined the sound of the nails being driven into Jesus' body. Taking communion more frequently made the crucifixion become more real to me. I will never take for granted or causally, the gift of salvation.

I knew this was the beginning of something. I was really wondering what in the world does God want to do with this. I was not convinced it was just a diet change. I often wished I would have just taken the wafer, shut my mouth, and walked away, *but* not me!

This all started with just a gluten-free diet that led to something else greater than what I could imagine, *The Wafer.* I realized that changing my diet meant changing the wafer. I remember in the very beginning, I briefly mentioned Monsanto to someone, and she responded, "Maybe you should protest." I thought for a moment, "She didn't even have a clue of what I was talking about. I am not protesting anything!"

Well, here I am ten years later. I am doing just that. But not Monsanto, I am protesting the **Protest**ants; the Christians. Yes, I said that, with boldness and confidence in the Lord. It is much easier to leave things the same and cling to the familiar, rather than stepping out in faith. I realized that for thirty-five years, I participated in Communion with little knowledge and a lack of desire. In my younger years, I just participated in Communion because it was what everyone else did. I was careless and ignorant about the whole process. I never stopped to ask any questions or to find out anything for myself. I certainly didn't want this wafer change to come from my opinion but rather God's plan. I was reminded of **Proverbs 18:2 (NIV)-** *Fools find no pleasure in understanding but delight in airing their own opinions.* I realize to some, this might be just foolish, but I know that God chose the foolish things, of the world, to shame the wise!

As I continued on, I later learned about the sacred raisin cakes, used to worship false gods and the Catholic doctrines. I then discovered the Law. The Code of Canon Law requires the wafer to be made from wheat and the newly revised version stipulates that it must be made with gluten. That is from the Code of Canon but what does the word of God say it should be made from? I spent much time in prayer and asked many questions concerning this matter. I had no idea where all this was leading to. I was just seeking God for His plan, purpose, and His will for my life. I desired to be all in and fully surrendered to Him. I knew this would not be done in my own strength or ability but by surrendering to His will! One thing I know full well is that no one can overthrow what is from God.

Without a solid understanding of God's revelation, how can we be sure that the spiritual influence we sense is truly from God? We have to maximize our dependence on the Holy Spirit. During one of my bible classes, Dr. Kelly stated, **"Don't allow other teachings of traditions, experiences, or reasons, hold above scripture"** This was an eye-opening awakening statement.

This whole journey would have been so much easier, for me, if God had come down with fire and brimstone; a burning bush moment, and said, **"DO NOT TAKE THAT WAFER."** In fact, I wished He had. Believe me, I have wanted to quit many times over. I wanted to eat the same as everyone else, I wanted to take the same wafer as everyone else. I didn't want to be different! I continued to beg, bargain, and pleaded with Him. But the answer to the gluten-free diet and wafer changes remained the same. After all my research and praying, I found it hard to offer a genetically modified wafer to a Holy God; a wafer made with gluten, with the name seitan, pronounced *satan*, created for Buddhist monks and endorsed by the Roman Catholic church. But here we stand, offering it to a Holy God. Satan has got to be laughing at this. Ask yourself, what's in your wafer? The devices and the wiles of the enemy found a way to get in. Just because this is my revelation, and my journey certainly doesn't mean you have to believe it. Have you ever wished you didn't ask a question before? Well, that was me, but I did, and I am glad that I did ask Him the question, and many other questions along the way. "What do you say?"

I asked God, "Is taking the wafer contradicting to my gluten-free lifestyle? Or is it contradicting not to partake of the traditional wafer that we use in Communion? I found myself at a major crossroads; a big intersection of decisions. What a place to be! If I could pick what I was called to do for Christ, certainly it would not have been this. I am grateful He chose me for the journey; although my flesh fought against it. My sole desire and my heart are to please and honor Christ. I have endured ten years on this long journey. If it was on my heart, I believe it is the heart of God, as we commune with Him, we will know Him more intimately.

I am thankful for the journey that led me closer to God. When we truly encounter Him, we will never be the same. As I come to a close, I pray that this has touched your heart in some way and encouraged you to go deeper in the secret place and discover the hidden mysteries of God's Word because there is so much to be revealed.

It was in the breaking of the bread that He was made known to me and my eyes were opened. I had a real awakening. He reminded me of the powerful scripture in John when Jesus said eat my flesh and drink of my blood. **John 6:56:** *Whoever eats My flesh and drinks My blood remains in Me, and I in him.* I had yet another powerful revelation from the understanding that in the Lord's Supper, Jesus was about to transition from flesh to spirit. The crucifixion and resurrection of Jesus Christ brought forth the gift of His Holy Spirit!

I want to challenge you to go deeper in God's Word. As you look over the reflections, begin to seek Him for the answers to your questions. His Word is alive and when it gets inside of us, we too can come alive in Christ. I challenge you to find Him in your secret place and allow the Holy Spirit to take you deeper with Him. Come now and dine with Him! **He is waiting for you!**

The Kidney Transplant

In the beginning, I was praying for a kidney for my husband. Then I lost my mother, and my world was falling apart. We later found out that gluten was potentially linked to David's original kidney disease. In the process, I held to the power of praying, fasting, and taking communion.

In the meantime, my husband's health continued to decline. I wondered if God kept me so consumed in Him to help me through my husband's sickness. I don't know if I could really express what was truly going on at the time. I fought, with everything inside me, praying that David would not be on dialysis. I prayed day and night, and night and day. I was on a never-ending fast, and eating Communion wafers several times a day.

The day came when David had to have a surgical procedure for the dialysis port. The very day of his surgery, I pulled up to let him out at the hospital door, while I went to park the car. I fussed at God with every step that I took. "Where are you, God? You took my Mama from me! I thought your timing was perfect." I prayed so fervently. I was so defeated and depleted. I walked in and sat down, while David was being prepped for surgery, not understanding how we got to this point.

I sat in that lobby, so hurt, angry, and lonely. A short while later, I received an alert from a text message. I thought to myself, "I do not want to talk to anyone right now." Well, the phone chimed again! I picked up my phone and the message read, "CALL ME!" I hesitated for a moment but called back. As soon as I said, "Hey", a very excited voice said, "I'm a MATCH!!!" I shouted, "WHAT???" and she replied, "Yes, I am a donor match; they just called me!" "Oh!" I began to shout; laughing and crying all at the same time. The next words that I heard, on the phone were, "God is always on time".

I jumped up and wanted to run to get David out of surgery. This can't be happening! Fortunately, following the surgery, David never received any form of dialysis. A few months later, he received an organ gift; a kidney from my maid-of-honor, my hero, our angel, Leslie Mitchell Lunsford. The very one that handed me my ring, on my wedding day, so selflessly handed my husband her kidney. God is faithful and answered our prayers! We will remain forever grateful!

Reflections

Reflections

1. Why do you take communion?

_____

_____

_____

2. Who was the queen of heaven mentioned in the book of Jeremiah?

_____

_____

_____

3. What are you doing in *Remembrance of Him* as you take the wafer?

_____

_____

_____

4. Are you participating in Communion as a way to commune with Him or just partaking as a ritual tradition?

_____

_____

_____

5. Who and what kind of image were they making cakes in?

_____

_____

6. In Hosea, how did they turn to other Gods and depart from the Lord?

_____

_____

_____

7. Have we taken those raisin cakes and brought them into Communion?

_____

_____

_____

_____

8. What did sacred raisin cakes have to do with making cakes for the Queen of Heaven, in relation to communion today?

_____

_____

_____

9. Why was Satan allowed into the Upper Room during The Lord's Supper?

_____

_____

_____

10. What did Jesus mean when He said, "Do what you come to do and do it quickly?"

_____

_____

_____

_____

11. Why did Satan enter Judas at the very moment he received the bread?

_____

_____

_____

_____

12. What happened to Satan and the bread when he left the Upper Room?

_____

_____

_____

13. Judas hung himself, but what did Satan do after he left?

_____

_____

_____

14. Why did the whole scene happen in the Upper Room during that time?

_____

_____

_____

_____

15. Have we completely separated from the Catholic religion/teaching?

_____

_____

_____

_____

16. Do we remain under Catholic Law with the use of the same wafer?

_____

_____

_____

OVERTURNING
the
TABLES

TERESA BARNHARDT

About the Author
Teresa Barnhardt

About the Author

Teresa Barnhardt is from Tarboro, North Carolina, but has made Rocky Mount her home for the past twelve years. She is a devoted wife and mother who enjoys nothing more than spending time with her family. Teresa has been married to David for twenty-three years and they have twin boys, Layton and Cayden, who are now in college.

Teresa has faced many challenges and twists and turns throughout her journey. It was during her studies that her book was birthed in the secret place.

Teresa is passionate about learning and teaching the Word of God. She has a heart to see others transformed by the love of God. Her desire is to see others set free of bondage and embrace their true identity and authority in Christ.

Teresa is a Certified Life Coach. She is an avid student and has spent the past eight years pursuing her education in Biblical Studies. She has a Masters in Christian Counseling and a Doctorate in Theology, Th.D. She obtained her ordination through Servants United in Ministry. Teresa is an active member of New Life Church in Rocky Mount, North Carolina.

Sources

GrowSeed.com

The Wheat Belly Dr. William Davis

Dr Mark Hyman

https://celiac.org

HealthyLiving.com

https://www.biblegateway.com

https://www.dictionary.com

Alba therapeutics.com

http://google.com

https://www.wikipedia.org

Dr Alessio Fasno

Beal, John P., et al. New Commentary on the Code of Canon Law. Paulist Press, 2000.

Batterson, M. (2012). *Praying circles around your children.* Zondervan.

Green, Thomas J. "Matter of Eucharist." New Commentary on the Code of Canon Law, Paulist Press, New York, 2000, pp. 1115–1116.

OVERTURNING
the
TABLES

TERESA BARNHARDT

Made in the USA
Middletown, DE
14 September 2023

38347000R00076